Guidelines for Writing a Qualitative Research Report

David Morris, Ph.D.
Associate Professor of Marketing
University of New Haven

STRUCTURE OF A QUALITATIVE RESEARCH REPORT

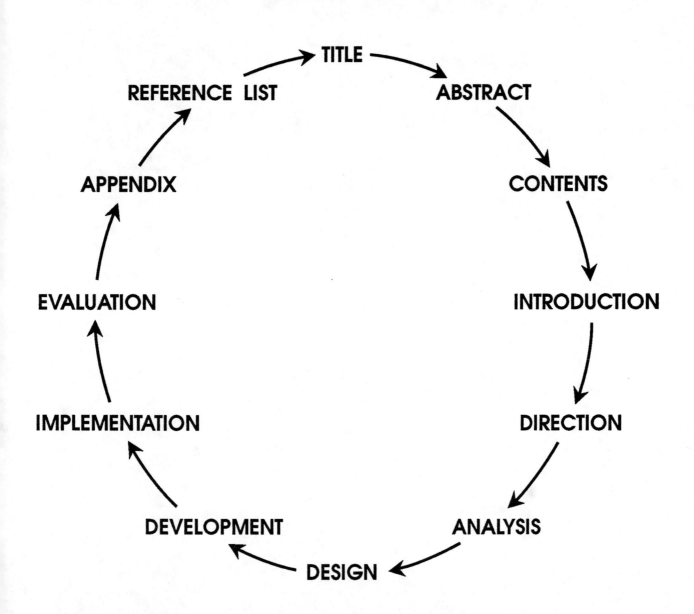

CONTENTS*

*This CONTENTS page has been limited to one page to save space.

FOREWORD

This book outlines the basic steps used in writing a qualitative research report. The process of ANALYSIS, DESIGN, DEVELOPMENT, IMPLEMENTATION, and EVALUATION (ADDIE) is a common process applied to both qualitative and quantitative research*. The differences are far fewer than the similarities when the ADDIE process is held constant. ADDIE is also applied in *Guidelines for Case Analysis.* Qualitative research does not rely on quantitative or mathematical measurements of proof. Qualitative research can be of great value to those who take the time to discover the insights it offers. This book explains the requirements in writing a qualitative research report. The author does not presume that his treatment of the subject is exhaustive. Unlike linearly designed texts, this book is designed with a circular ADDIE model to give the learner a quick and broad understanding of the topic. The *Guidelines* is not meant to replace any text on qualitative research. It is an overview of a research process which can be developed through time and experience. White space is provided for notes.

The book contains few samples of qualitative research because it is designed to deal with landmarks of structure applying the ADDIE process. Use the "Structure of a Qualitative Research Report" charts as a template to assess your research project. The research community employs many different types of qualitative research. Thus, the learner should try to explore new areas. Although the author does not reject quantification as valueless, he does not accept it as the supreme method to achieve understanding. We learn from all forms of experience. The philosophies we develop and acquire affect our response to the world. We are all the children of our philosophies.

D. Morris

*See *Guidelines for Writing a Research Report.*

STRUCTURE OF A QUALITATIVE RESEARCH REPORT

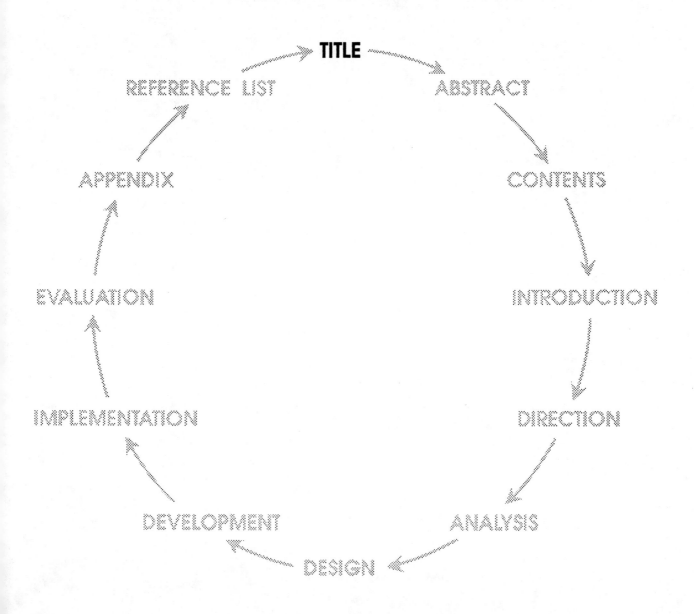

TITLE PAGE

The TITLE page should contain the following:

The TITLE of the Research Project

The TITLE of the research project should identify the nature and scope of the project.

Capitalize the first letter of the first word in the TITLE, of the first letter of the first word following a colon, and of all other words excluding articles, coordinating conjunctions and prepositions.

Author Identification

Identify yourself and other members of your team by name and designation.

Names may be listed either in alphabetical order or according to the amount of contribution.

Designation refers to the title(s) of the researcher(s).

Address and telephone number may be included.

Examples:

Richard Plank, Ph.D.

David Kimball, Sc.D.
Assistant Professor of Marketing

Barbara Cavallaro
Researcher

Identification of Sponsoring Organization(s)

In circumstances where the research project is conducted for a particular professor or organization, or funded by a sponsor, the name of such individual or organization should be included.

The identification should be preceded by a phrase such as

Submitted to

Prepared for

Presented at

Date

The Date of the final submission or final preparation of the project.

Use *The Chicago Manual of Style* for the layout of the TITLE page.
See next page for an example of a TITLE page.
A TITLE page should not be numbered.

Interviews with Chief Executive Officers:
Their Perceptions of Marketing

by

David Morris, Ph.D.
Associate Professor of Marketing
University of New Haven
300 Orange Avenue
West Haven, CT 06516
(203) 932-7348

Submitted to

Journal of Marketing

May 1998

The above is an example a TITLE page.

STRUCTURE OF A QUALITATIVE RESEARCH REPORT

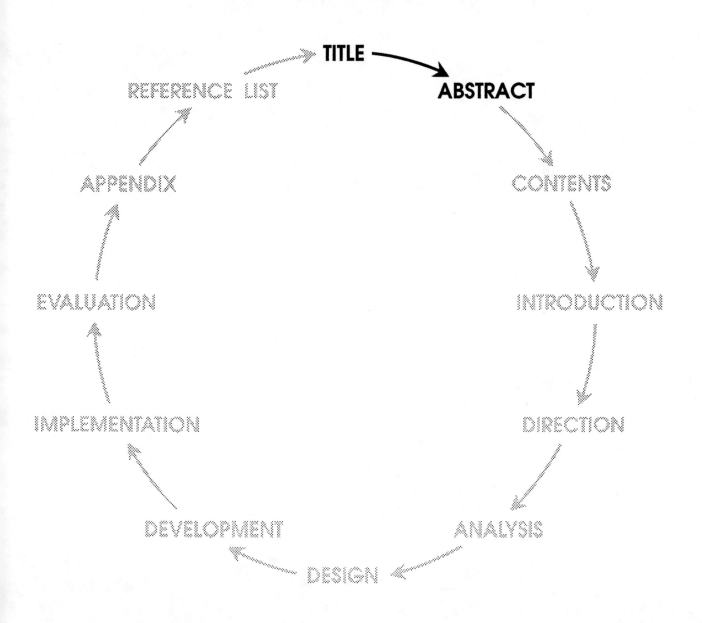

ABSTRACT

The ABSTRACT in a qualitative research report should contain:

The nature of the research.

> An identification of the general area of study (for example, leadership).

The scope of the project.

> The parameters of the project (for example, leadership's perception of marketing).

The methodology used in the project (for example, interview, historic, case study).

Conclusions and recommendations.

The ABSTRACT:

Is used when the document is published as a general overview.

Gives the reader a quick overview.

Should cover from one-fourth to one-third of a page.

Is written after the project is completed.

Is organized into one paragraph.

Appears on a separate page, numbered in a lowercase Roman numeral, with the word "ABSTRACT" centered at the top.

Is single-spaced.

STRUCTURE OF A QUALITATIVE RESEARCH REPORT

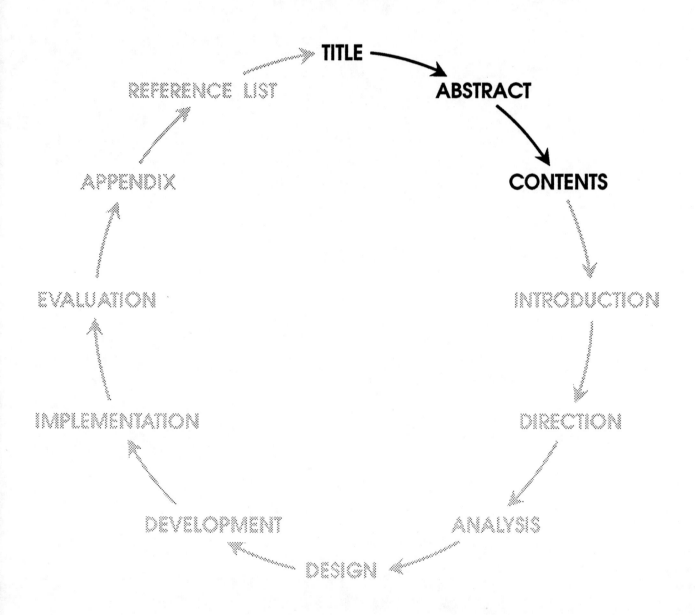

CONTENTS

The CONTENTS assists the reader in finding relevant materials in the research report.

The CONTENTS contains the following items and their page numbers:

The CONTENTS also includes subsections and their page numbers.

The subjects of the APPENDICES may be included in the CONTENTS or on a separate page. The first page of the APPENDIX is numbered in sequence with the other pages in the CONTENTS. Specific APPENDIX references are numbered A-1, A-2, A-3, etc. This may be done for each page in the APPENDIX or for each document in the AP-PENDIX. Other pages in the APPENDIX may be numbered B-1, B-2, B-3 or C-1, C-2, etc. (p. 31).

See *The Chicago Manual of Style* for more details.
The CONTENTS page or pages are numbered in lower-case Roman numerals.

STRUCTURE OF A QUALITATIVE RESEARCH REPORT

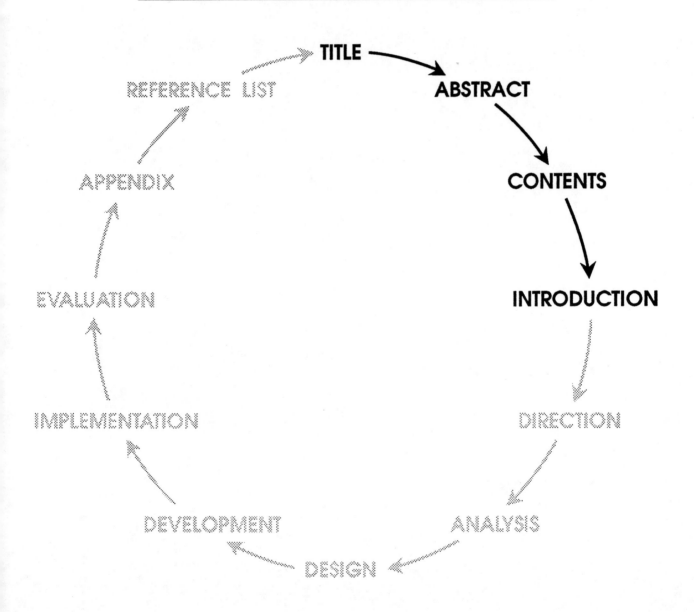

INTRODUCTION

The INTRODUCTION provides a broader view of the research report than the ABSTRACT.

As a rule, the INTRODUCTION should not exceed two pages. However, the length of the document determines the length of the INTRODUCTION.

The INTRODUCTION is most effective when written after the report is completed.

The INTRODUCTION should include:

> The historical background of the subject.

> A description and justification of the methodology employed.

> A broad interpretation of the findings or results.

The text pages begin with Arabic numeral 1.

STRUCTURE OF A QUALITATIVE RESEARCH REPORT

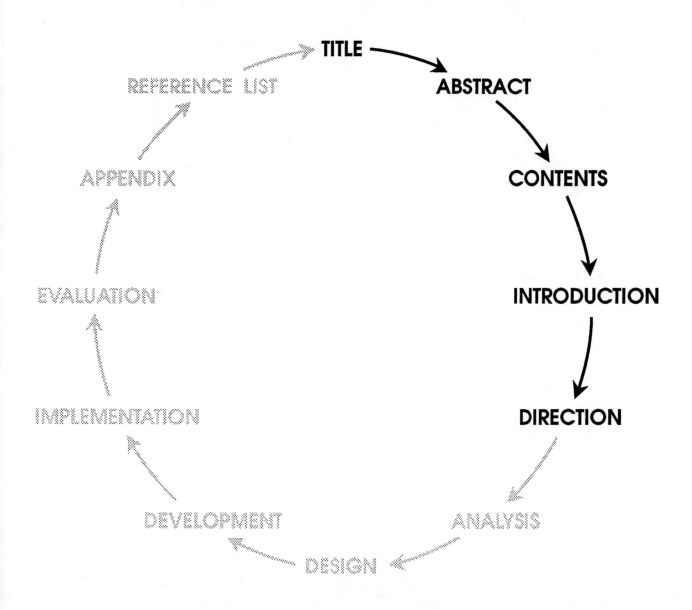

DIRECTION

The concept of the DIRECTION, or purpose, of a study is researcher specific. The DIRECTION, end, or purpose of qualitative research can range from being very precise and well-defined (deductive) to open, with no definition (inductive). The researcher must specify the approach in the DIRECTION section of the report (p. 13).

The purpose of qualitative research is to explore a subject in order to increase understanding. What will be found is more open to researcher interpretation. This may be viewed as one of the distinct advantages of qualitative research.

Quantitative research is directed at verifying, refuting, and developing theories of explanation and prediction. Mathematical verification is the method used to determine the outcomes.* If a theory is not mathematically verified, even though the study has been done correctly, the theory is not supported. New theories should be put forth to explain and predict. See *Guidelines for Writing a Research Report.*

The underlying assumptions that explain and predict in qualitative research apply nonmathematical evidence. Qualitative research has been viewed by some quantitative researchers as a first step in the process of mathematical verification. Qualitative research does not have to be a first step in quantitative research. Qualitative research can be an end in itself. Life gives us more opportunities for explanation and prediction than the advocates of the mathematical position would admit. Both qualitative and quantitative research, however, are just two of many world views that we can choose to reject or accept at this time in history.

---

*This statement should not suggest that the questions in qualitative research may not be precise. Questions are derived from the DIRECTION.

The DIRECTION section contains the DIRECTION or Purpose of the Research Study and the DIRECTION Statement:

The DIRECTION or Purpose of the Research Study:

> Defines the study's general purpose.
>
> Justifies the study's organization.
>
> Describes what the study is expected to accomplish.

The DIRECTION Statement must:

> Have its own heading.
>
> Be clearly stated.
>
> Be written in one sentence.
>
> Determine the research question(s).
>
> Set the direction of all research to follow.

DIRECTION OR PURPOSE OF THE STUDY

This DIRECTION is similar to the statement of the problem in quantitative research. The approach to qualitative research is process-oriented rather than problem-oriented.

DIRECTION STATEMENT

State the DIRECTION in one sentence.

STRUCTURE OF A QUALITATIVE RESEARCH REPORT

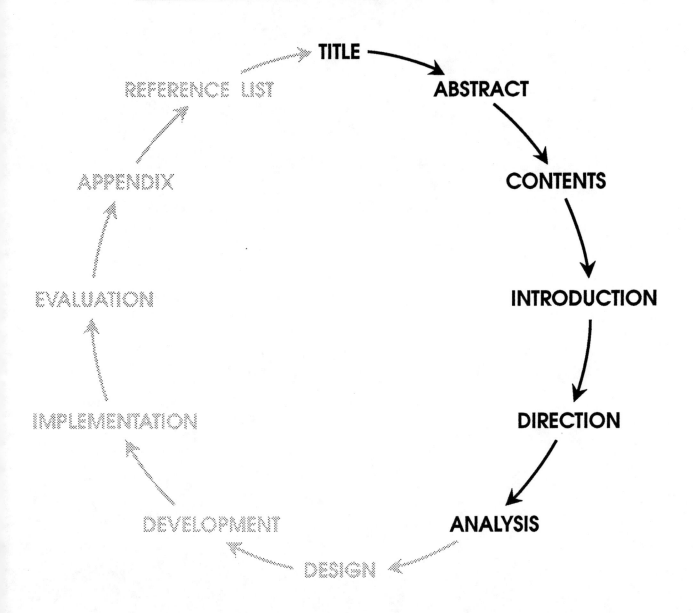

ANALYSIS

The ANALYSIS step of the ADDIE qualitative research process involves gathering data or information to achieve a DIRECTION, end, or purpose.

TYPES OF STUDY

Four Types of Studies may be applied to qualitative research:

Exploratory

> Explore, survey, examine, investigate.

Explanatory

> Explain, illuminate, decipher, reveal, resolve, illustrate, interpret, demonstrate, define.

Descriptive

> Describe, characterize, delineate, portray, narrate, relate, report.

Predictive

> Predict, forecast, project, prognosticate, anticipate, prophesize.

METHODS

Several Methods may be employed to gather information to achieve a DIRECTION in qualitative research.

Historical Research

Life Histories

continued on next page

METHODS (continued)

    Extrapolation

    Case Studies

    Current Surveys

    Causal Studies

    A Point of View or Experience

    Religious Experience

    Philosophy

    Language (Written, oral, nonverbal)

    Interviews

    Participant Observations

    Language Content Analysis

    Literature Review

    Projective Techniques

    Field Studies

    Logical Inference

    Myths

    Ethnographic Analysis

    Others

Match the Type of Study with the specific Method to achieve a DIRECTION in the DESIGN (p. 21).

PRIMARY/SECONDARY SOURCES

Primary Sources

The researcher gathers this information firsthand.

Secondary Sources

The researcher gathers this data from other sources.

Both Primary and Secondary Sources are used to achieve a purpose. The distinction between primary and secondary sources depends on the study. For example, if one is looking for a primary source for the writings of Aristotle, *The Complete Works Of Aristotle* edited by Jonathan Barnes would not be appropriate. The text written by Aristotle in Greek is required. If it did not exist, the sources would be secondary.

The text by Barnes can also be a primary source if the subject of the study is this specific edition of Aristotle's works.

The types of sources depend on the DIRECTION and how the study has been framed (p. 13).

QUESTIONS

The Questions are derived from the DIRECTION or Purpose of the Study and the DIRECTION Statement (p. 13).

State clearly the Questions which the study wishes to answer. If the study is exploratory, then ask exploratory questions (p. 15).

The answers to these Questions represent the outcome of the research project.

The Questions should be stated in a way that their answers can be supported or refuted by the study. The answers to the Questions will be elaborated on in the Discussion section of EVALUATION (p. 29).

The Questions must be answerable within the time and cost set for the project.

The researcher must have realistic expectations for the project:

> For example, I might like to do an in-depth interview with President Clinton, but he is more than likely unavailable to me for this purpose.

REVIEW OF THE LITERATURE

> Review previous and current projects (qualitative and quantitative) on similar subjects.

> Evaluate similar literature and discuss the Type of Study and the Methods that were employed (pp. 15, 16).

DEFINITIONS

Define the terms which, to the reader, may be unfamiliar. Consult *Webster's Third New International Dictionary* and/or scholarly publications. Give credit to your sources.

You may define your own terms. Keep the Definitions consistent throughout your report.

STRUCTURE OF A QUALITATIVE RESEARCH REPORT

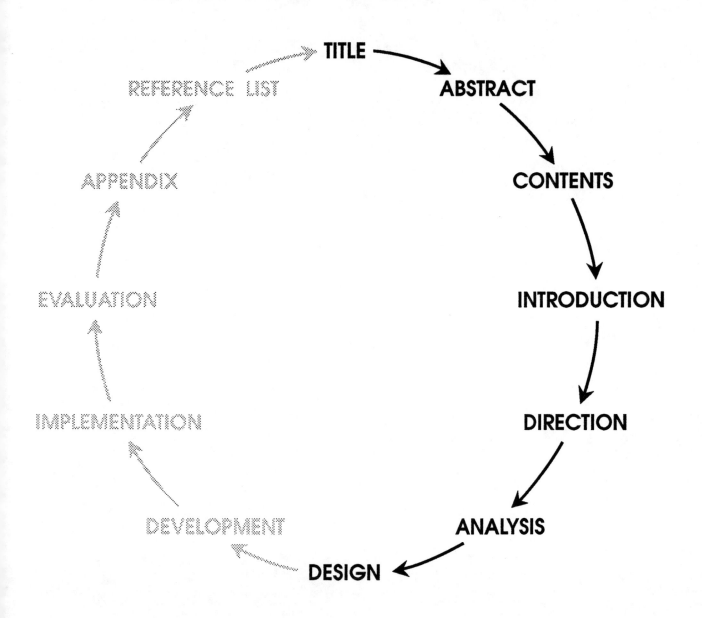

DESIGN

The DESIGN describes how the research project is to be carried out.

Having identified the DIRECTION or Purpose of the Research and performed the ANALYSIS, the researcher describes in the DESIGN how that DIRECTION is to be achieved.

SELECTED TYPE OF STUDY

Studies may be exploratory, explanatory, descriptive, or predictive. Explain why you have chosen a particular Type of Study (p. 15).

METHOD(S) EMPLOYED IN THE STUDY

The selection of the DESIGN is based on the type of research Method(s) that are selected to achieve the DIRECTION of the study (pp. 15, 16). Discuss the Method(s) you have chosen and the reason(s) for that choice.

APPLICATION OF METHOD(S)

Once the research Method(s) have been selected, the DESIGN employs one or more of the following applications to achieve the DIRECTION:

> Compare, Contrast, Sequence, Combine, Separate, Order, Converge, Match, Measure, Weigh, Cycle, Link, Count, Dictate, Number, Measure, Classify, Index, Assemble, Grade, Transpose, Rank, Reproduce, Copy, Question, Join, Merge, Consolidate, Itemize, Chronologize, etc.

Justify the selection of particular application(s) to achieve your DIRECTION.

STUDY

Describe the Study—its Scope, Sample Size, Data, Data Collection, Validity, Reliability, Cost Benefit, and Limitations.

SCOPE OF STUDY

Identify the parameters of the Study; no Study can be all things to all people.

DATA

Data is loosely defined as the information applied to achieve a purpose. Data does not need to have a numerical orientation.

DATA COLLECTION

How are you going to acquire and organize the data to achieve a DIRECTION?

CAUSE AND EFFECT

The relationship between Cause and Effect has been a critical component in Western thinking since the sixteenth century. Before then, all causes were attributed to the First Cause, God. Many research studies attempt to show a Cause and Effect relationship based on a secular understanding of the world. Quantitative research maintains that Cause and Effect can be demonstrated only through mathematical means. Qualitative research demonstrates this relationship through other means. Qualitative research has some mathematical applications, but relationships do not have to be verified mathematically.

When appropriate, discuss how your research will show a Cause and Effect relationship.

VALIDITY

The extent to which a conclusion is a true reflection of the data.

While questionnaires have been applied to quantitative research, the DESIGN issue should be discussed in broader terms in qualitative research. Why should the reader believe that your study represents an accurate reflection of the results?

RELIABILITY

The extent to which the same data could be generated/replicated by another researcher.

For example, if I were to measure the space which a newspaper gives over time to a specific issue, would someone else making the same study arrive at the same measurement? How did I avoid researcher error?

COST/BENEFIT

All studies incur Costs, but projected Costs of a Study should not exceed the Benefits. The Costs may be outlined under this heading.

LIMITATIONS

The researcher should identify the limits of the study in terms of time, money, personnel, and other factors. The budget may be discussed at this point. A complete budget should appear in the APPENDIX.

STRUCTURE OF A QUALITATIVE RESEARCH REPORT

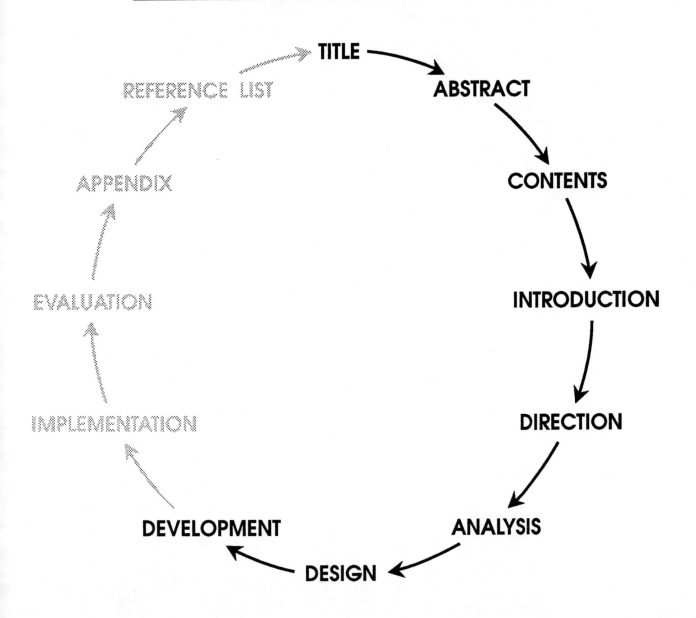

DEVELOPMENT

DEVELOPMENT

The DEVELOPMENT step involves the testing to show that the DESIGN will lead to the designated purpose or DIRECTION.

PILOT TESTING

There are several methods for testing the Study. Try out the DESIGN on a limited basis. Look at all aspects of the research and attempt to identify those areas that can be improved. Are they contributing to the DIRECTION in the best possible way? If they are not, then make the improvements.*

EXPERT (ASSISTANCE)

Another form of testing is to share your ideas with Experts and to solicit their contributions. If you have discussed the study with an Expert, give the reader this information. Cite it in the REFERENCE LIST (p. 33).

*See *Marketing as a Means to Achieve Organizational Ends.*

STRUCTURE OF A QUALITATIVE RESEARCH REPORT

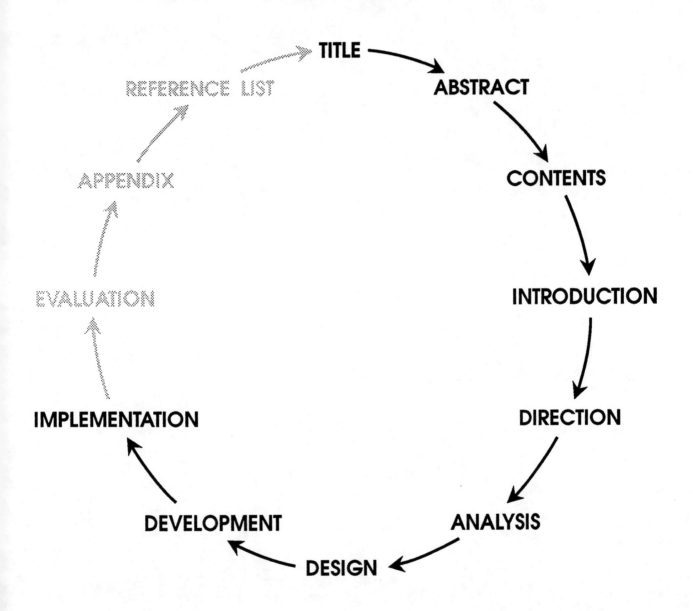

IMPLEMENTATION

Do the study as outlined in the DESIGN and DEVELOPMENT steps.

SUMMARY OF PROCEDURES

This section does not contain any value judgments; it simply states what was done and what was found.

This material is presented in logical form and sequence, which are held constant throughout the study.

Do not describe every detail of the study in IMPLEMENTATION. Select the key components that could have an impact on the findings.

Save the other details in your files because they may become valuable for further research. In some cases, put them in the APPENDIX.

SUMMARY OF FINDINGS

What did you find in the research report?

Explain the findings in as much detail as necessary for the reader to understand; too much is better than too little. If it is a short report, then give a representative example of the findings.

STRUCTURE OF A QUALITATIVE RESEARCH REPORT

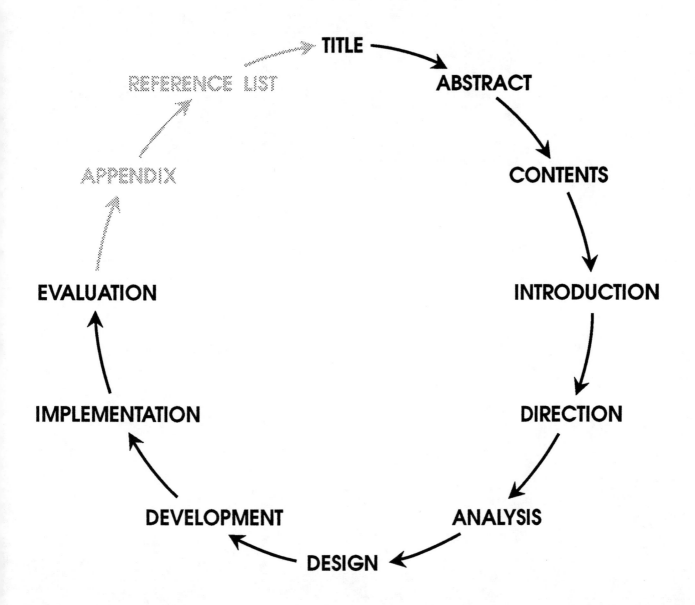

EVALUATION

The term EVALUATION is interchangeable with summary, conclusion, and/or findings.

DISCUSSION

Discuss each of the questions asked in the ANALYSIS (p. 17) in the same order.

The researchers Discuss the findings. They are free to interject their own beliefs and opinions. This section is subjective, because of "the myth of objectivity": Two researchers may view the exact same circumstance and come to entirely different conclusions. Is the glass half full or half empty?

RECOMMENDATIONS

The researchers, based on the findings, may recommend certain actions.

FURTHER RESEARCH

The researchers can propose other studies that would support and add to the same DIRECTION within the constraints of Costs and Benefits.

STRUCTURE OF A QUALITATIVE RESEARCH REPORT

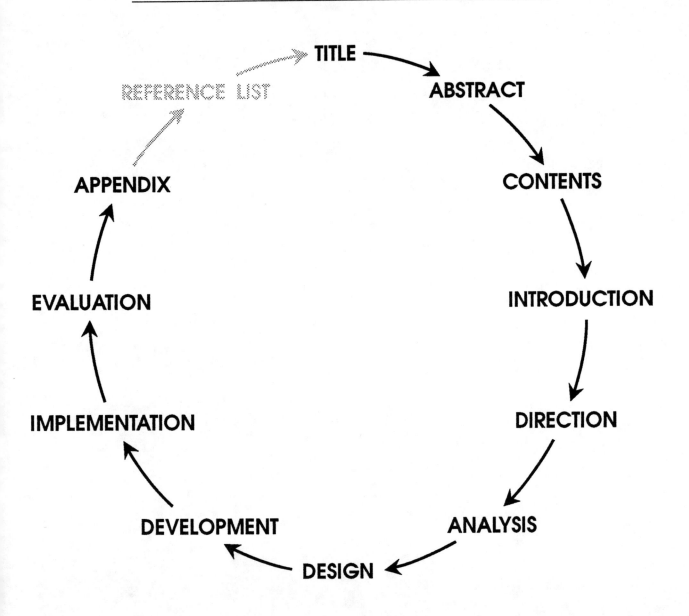

APPENDIX

The APPENDIX includes support materials that are not displayed in the text of the report. At the appropriate location in the text, the reader is informed that the materials are available in the APPENDIX (A-1, A-2, etc.).

The APPENDIX does not include raw data.

The APPENDIX may include the following items:

> Sample survey questions
>
> Charts
>
> Tables
>
> Illustrations
>
> Summary data
>
> Letters
>
> Interview questions and answers
>
> Documents

When appearing in the APPENDIX, these items are given a letter and a number (A-1, A-2, A-3 and B-1, B-2, etc.). Each item in the APPENDIX of the study must be identified. Check *The Chicago Manual of Style* for specific applications.

Major materials should appear in the text of the research report, not in the APPENDIX. The APPENDIX contains secondary support materials.

STRUCTURE OF A QUALITATIVE RESEARCH REPORT

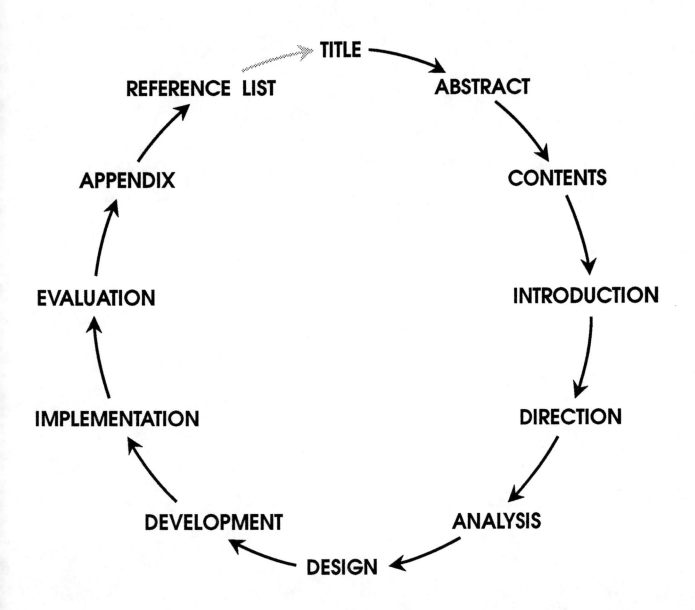

REFERENCE LIST

Style Manuals

Several Style Manuals are available to researchers writing a qualitative research report.

When paragraphs are summarized, or the text of another writer is quoted, the accepted form of citation must be used. Plagiarism is a serious issue.

For an in-depth review of the methods for REFERENCING, consult the *Guidelines for Business Writing* and *The Chicago Manual of Style*.

Ahmed, Saad, and David Morris. 1991. *Guidelines for business writing*. West Haven, Conn.: University of New Haven Press.

Barnes, Jonathan, ed. 1984. *The complete works of Aristotle*. Vol. 1, Princeton: Princeton University Press.

Morris, David. 1992. *Marketing as a means to achieve organizational ends*. 3rd ed. West Haven, Conn.: University of New Haven Press.

Morris, David, and Satish Chandra. 1993. *Guidelines for writing a research report*. Chicago: American Marketing Association.

_____. 1993. *Guidelines for case analysis*. Chicago: American Marketing Association.

University of Chicago Press. 1982. *The Chicago Manual of Style*. 13th ed. Chicago: University of Chicago Press.